POEMS
of
COMFORT
AND BLESSING

Compiled by

J. DANSON SMITH

Author of

"100 Best Loved Poems", "Songs in the Night" etc.

D1650166

Published by

B. McCALL BARBOUR
28 George IV Bridge, Edinburgh EH1 1ES, Scotland

First Edition

(in this style)

1976

© B. McCall Barbour

ISBN 0 7132 0023 5

Made and Printed in Great Britain by
Stanley L. Hunt (Printers) Ltd, Midland Road, Rushden, Northants

"IT IS JESUS"

By ANNIE JOHNSON FLINT

———

" And all the city was moved, saying, Who is this? . . . the multitude said, This is Jesus."—Matt. xxi. 10, 11.

———

THERE is a Voice through Earth's wild clamour calling,
  To all the heavy-laden and oppressed,
Sweet as the cooling dew at even falling;
  " Come unto Me and rest."

  It is the voice of Jesus still entreating,
    To all the comfortless and all the sad;
  Day after day His tender call repeating,
    " Come unto Me and I will make you glad."

There is a Hand outstretched in tenderest pity,
  Where all the weary and the wandering roam,
Waiting to lead them to the heavenly city,
  To bring the homeless Home.

  It is the hand of Jesus, still upholding;
  Strong to deliver, mighty still to keep:
  And none shall pluck from out that safe enfolding,
    The weakest one of all His blood-bought sheep.

There is a Form that walks life's stormy
    ocean,
  Bidding the noise of wind and tempest
    cease,
Crying aloud through all the wild commotion,
  " In Me ye shall have peace."

    Oh, it is Jesus, coming o'er the waters,
      As once He walked the waves of
        Galilee,—
    Speaking to all earth's shipwrecked sons
      and daughters,
      " Be not afraid; have faith, have
        faith in Me."

There is a Love that longs, with deep
    affection,
  To gather all the sin-sick sons of men
Beneath its wings of shelter and protection,
  And give them health again.

    It is the love of Jesus, sweet with longing
      His full salvation to the world to
        give,—
    Crying to all the dead, earth's highways
      thronging,
      " Come unto Me, come unto Me, and
        live."

Reprinted by special permission of
Evangelical Publishers, Toronto, Canada.

" A GOD WHO CARES "

By HUGH MILLER

" WHAT can it mean ? Is it aught to
Him
That the days are long, and the
nights are dim ?
Can He be touched by the griefs I bear,
Which sadden the heart and whiten the hair ?
About His throne are eternal calms,
And strong glad music of happy psalms,
And bliss unruffled by any strife—
How can HE care for *my* little life ?

And yet, I want Him to care for me,
While I live in this world where sorrows be.
When the lights die down from the path I
take ;
When strength is feeble and friends forsake ;
And love and music which once did bless,
Have left me to silence and loneliness,
Then my life-song changes to sobbing prayers,
And my heart cries out for a GOD WHO
CARES.

When shadows hang o'er the whole day long,
And my spirit is bowed with shame and
wrong,
And I am not good, and the bitter shade
Of conscious sin makes my soul afraid ;

And the busy world has too much to do
To stay in its courses to help me through ;
And I long for a Saviour—can it be
That the God of the universe CARES FOR
    ME ?

Oh, wonderful story of deathless Love,
Each child is dear to that heart above !
He fights for me when I cannot fight ;
He comforts me in the gloom of night ;
He lifts the burden, for He is strong ;
He stills the sigh and awakes the song ;
The sorrows that bear me down HE shares,
And loves and pardons because HE CARES.

Let all who are sad take heart again ;
We are not alone in our hours of pain :
Our Father looks from His throne above
To soothe and comfort us with His love.
He leaves us not when the storms are high,
And we have safety, for He is nigh ;
Can that be trouble which He doth share ?
Oh, rest in peace, for the Lord DOES
    CARE ! ''

" HIGHEST SERVICE "

CHRIST never asks of us such busy labour
    As leaves no time for resting at His
    feet ;
The waiting attitude of expectation
    He oft-times counts a service most com-
    plete.

He sometimes wants our ear, our rapt
    attention,
    That He some sweetest secret may impart ;
'Tis often in the time of deepest silence,
    That heart finds deepest fellowship with
    heart.

We sometimes wonder why our Lord doth
    place us
    Within a sphere so narrow, so obscure,
That nothing we call work can find an
    entrance ;
    There's only room to suffer, to endure.

Well, God loves patience.   Souls that dwell
    in stillness,
    Doing the little things, or resting quite,
May just as perfectly fulfil their mission,
    Be just as useful in the Father's sight,

As they who grapple with some giant evil,
    Clearing a path, that every eye may see.
Our Saviour cares for cheerful acquiescence,
    Rather than for a busy ministry.

And yet, He does love service, where 'tis
        given
    By grateful love that clothes itself in deed ;
But work that's done beneath the scourge of
        duty,
    Be sure, He gives to such but little heed.

Then seek to please Him, whatsoe'er He bids
        thee,
    Whether to do, to suffer, or lie still ;
'Twill matter little by what path He led us,
    If in it all we sought to do His will.

—Anon.

" HE'S HELPING ME NOW "

By ANNIE JOHNSON FLINT

———

" *A very present help.*"—Psalm xlvi. 1.

———

HE'S helping me now—this moment,
　　Though I may not see it or hear,—
　　Perhaps by a friend far distant,—
　Perhaps by a stranger near ;
Perhaps by a spoken message,—
　Perhaps by the printed word ;
In ways that I know and know not
　I have the help of the Lord.

He's keeping me now—this moment,
　However I need it most,—
Perhaps by a single angel,
　Perhaps by a mighty host ;
Perhaps by the chain that frets me,—
　Or the walls that shut me in :
In ways that I know and know not
　He keeps me from harm and sin.

He's guiding me now—this moment,
　In pathways easy or hard ;
Perhaps by a door wide open,
　Perhaps by a door fast barred ;

Perhaps by a joy withholden,—
　Perhaps by a gladness given ;
In ways that I know and know not
　He's leading me up to Heaven.

He's using me now—this moment,
　And whether I go or stand,
Perhaps by a plan accomplished,—
　Perhaps when He stays my hand ;
Perhaps by a word in season,
　Perhaps by a silent prayer ;
In ways that I know and know not
　His labour of love I share.

By per. Evangelical Publishers.

"IS IT TRUE?"

"I know the thoughts that I think toward you, saith the Lord, thoughts of peace, and not of evil, to give you an expected end."
—Je. xxix. 11.

"He leadeth me beside the still waters."
—Ps. xxiii. 2.

"I will fear no evil: for Thou art with me."—Ps. xxiii. 4.

" IS it true that my Saviour is planning
    for me,
    When the way is rough and long,
And the clouds hang low and friends are few,
    And I have no voice for song?

Is it true He is planning my whole life
    through,
    Each moment, from day to day?
Does He love and care enough for me
    To listen to all I say? "

" Yes! He's silently planning, dear one, for
    you,
    When the days are long and drear,
He loves, and He cares so much for you,
    Take courage and banish all fear.

He is planning the very best for you
    Through tedious days of strife,
Just trust and cling close to that Blessèd One
    In the ups and downs of life."

—*Selected.*

" WIT'S END CORNER "

By ANTOINETTE WILSON

*" They reel to and fro . . . and are at their
wit's end. Then they cry unto the* LORD *in
their trouble, and He bringeth them out of their
distresses."*—Psalm cvii. 27, 28.

ARE you standing at " Wit's End
Corner,"
 Christian with troubled brow ?
Are you thinking of what is before you,
 And all you are bearing now ?
Does all the world seem against you,
 Are you in the battle alone ?
Remember—at " Wit's End Corner "
 Is just where God's power is shown.

Are you standing at " Wit's End Corner,"
 Blinded with wearying pain,
Feeling you cannot endure it,
 You cannot bear the strain,
Bruised through the constant suffering,
 Dizzy, and dazed, and numb ?
Remember—to " Wit's End Corner,"
 Is where Jesus loves to come !

Are you standing at " Wit's End Corner,"
 Your work before you spread,
All lying, begun, unfinished,
 And pressing on heart and head,

Longing for strength to do it,
  Stretching out trembling hands?
Remember—at " Wit's End Corner "
  The Burden-bearer stands.

Are you standing at " Wit's End Corner,"
  Yearning for those you love,
Longing and praying and watching,
  Pleading their cause above,
Trying to lead them to Jesus,
  Wond'ring if you've been true?
He whispers, " At Wit's End Corner,
  I'll win them, as I won you ! "

Are you standing at " Wit's End Corner " ?
  Then you're just in the very spot
To learn the wondrous resources
  Of Him who faileth not !
No doubt to a brighter pathway
  Your footsteps will soon be moved,
But only at " Wit's End Corner "
  Is " the God who is able " proved !

" THE UNKNOWN MORROW "

By Rev. Frank J. Exley, D.D.

CHILD of My love, fear not the unknown
    morrow,
    Dread not the new demand life makes
      of thee ;
Thy ignorance doth hold no cause for sorrow,
    Since what thou knowest not is known to
      Me.

Thou canst not see to-day the hidden meaning
    Of My command, but thou the light shalt
      gain ;
Walk on in faith, upon My promise leaning,
    And as thou goest all shall be made plain.

One step thou seest—then go forward boldly,
    One step is far enough for faith to see ;
Take that, and thy next duty shall be told
    thee,
    For, step by step, thy Lord is leading thee.

Stand not in fear, thy adversaries counting ;
    Dare every peril, save to disobey ;
Thou shalt march on, all obstacles surmount-
    ing,
    For I, the Strong, will open up the way.

Wherefore go gladly to the task assigned
    thee,—
    Having My promise, needing nothing more
Than just to know, where'er the future finds
    thee,
    In all thy journeying I go before.

" ONLY A LITTLE SPARROW "

I AM only a little sparrow !
    A bird of low degree :
My life is of little value,
    But the dear Lord cares for me.

He gave me a coat of feathers,—
    'Tis very plain, I know :
With never a speck of crimson,
    For it was not made for show.

But, it keeps me warm in winter,
    It shields me from the rain ;
Were it bordered with gold and purple
    Perhaps it would make me vain.

And now, when the springtime cometh,
    I will build me a little nest,
With many a chirp and flutter,
    In the spot I love the best.

I have no barn or storehouse ;
    I never sow nor reap :
God gives me a sparrow's portion,—
    But never a seed to keep.

If my meat is sometimes scanty,
    Close picking makes it sweet :
I have always enough to keep me,—
    And " Life is more than meat."

I know there are many sparrows ;
　　All over the world they're found :
But our Heavenly Father knoweth
　　When one of us falls to the ground.

Though small, we are never forgotten,—
　　Though weak, we are never afraid,—
For we know that the dear Lord keepeth
　　The lives of the creatures He made.

I fly through the thickest forest,—
　　I light on many a spray,—
I have no chart or compass,
　　But, I never lose my way.

　　　　　　　　　　—Anon.

" JUST FOR TO-DAY "

LORD, for to-morrow and its needs,
  I do not pray ;
 Keep me, my God, from stain of sin,
  Just for to-day.

Let me both diligently work,
  And duly pray ;
Let me be kind in word and deed,
  Just for to-day.

Let me be slow to urge my will,
  Prompt to obey ;
Help me to mortify my flesh,
  Just for to-day.

Let me no wrong or idle word
  Unthinking say ;
Set Thou a seal upon my lips,
  Just for to-day.

Lo, for to-morrow and its needs,
  I do not pray—
But keep me, guide me, love me, Lord,
  Just for to-day.

       —Anon.

" IT'S ALL RIGHT ! "
By B. M'Call Barbour

SIMPLE words, so simply spoken
　　That they seem mere commonplace,
　Yet to weary hearts, nigh broken,
　Fraught with God's own blessèd peace.

" It's all right ! " though disappointment
　Casts a cloud across our way,
All things are together bringing
　Us unto God's " perfect day."

" It's all right ! " when friends mistake us,
　When they do not understand,
Oh, how sweet to know all's guided
　By our heavenly Father's hand.

" It's all right ! "　How long I heard it,
　" God has *all* your sins forgiven.
Jesus died for your deliverance,
　And He made a way to heaven."

" It's all right ! "　I just believed it,
　And I trusted His sweet word,
I accepted His salvation,
　Now I'm resting in the Lord.

" It's all right ! "　Yes, now I know it,
　More is right than first I thought,
All is right, for I have Jesus,
　He has for me all things wrought.

" It's all right ! "   I've peace that's perfect,
   I've a joy no tongue can tell,
I've the very love of Jesus,
   And His very life as well.

" It's all right ! "   We will believe it,
   Not because we " ought " or " must,"
But because we cannot doubt it,
   We can only love and trust.

" It's all right ! " though death surrounds us,
   Though our dearest hopes are crushed,
Though our prayers remain unanswered,
   And our hearts laid in the dust.

" It's all right ! "   Yes, Lord, we'll say it,
   Though Thou slayest, as we say ;
" It's all right ! "   the Hand that gave us
   Will not wrongly take away.

" It's all right ! "   Yes, He is living,
   I am conqueror in His might ;
" Self " has found its grave in Jesus,
   And I know " it is all right."

So we learn to know Him better,
   So we come to trust Him quite,
When in praise and peaceful patience,
   We just say, " Yes, Lord, all right ! "

" HE GIVETH MORE GRACE "

By ANNIE JOHNSON FLINT

HE giveth more grace when the burdens
    grow greater,
    He sendeth more strength when the
    labours increase ;
To added affliction He addeth His mercies,
    To multiplied trials His multiplied peace.

When we have exhausted our store of
    endurance,
    When our strength has failed ere the day is
    half done,
When we reach the end of our hoarded
    resources,
    Our Father's full giving is only begun.

His love has no limit, His grace has no
    measure,
    His power no boundary known unto men ;
For out of His infinite riches in Jesus
    He giveth and giveth and giveth again.

By per. Evangelical Publishers, Toronto.

"HE FAILETH NOT"
By Edwin R. Miles

EACH happy morn when I awake,
This promise for the day I take,
" I'll never leave thee, nor forsake,"
He faileth not.

How sweet His word unto my soul,
To cleanse from sin and make me whole,
To cheer, encourage and console,
He faileth not.

Along life's road I'll fear no ill,
For Christ my Lord is with me still,
He *never* failed !   He never *will* !
He faileth not.

In daily cares and troubles sore,
When Satan tempts me, o'er and o'er,
His promise stands for evermore,
He faileth not.

When dark the days and drear the skies,
And often bitter trials rise,
When all else fails, my faith then cries,
He faileth not.

He bears my burdens, carries, too,
My cares and sorrows, all life through,
How good the promise, and how true,
He faileth not.

He has not failed me in the past,
He will not fail while life shall last,
For wheresoe'er my lot is cast,
                He faileth not.

The Saviour's coming from above,
To take me to His home of love,
His promise I shall faithful prove,
                He faileth not.

And when I reach that golden shore,
My trouble and my labour o'er,
I'll sing this song for evermore,
                He FAILED not.

"LO, I AM WITH YOU!"

By J. DANSON SMITH

"Lo, I am with you!" Statement so
blest!
　Full of such wonderful comfort and
　　rest!
Balm for the sorrowing ; cheer for the sad ;
Light for the desolate—light that makes
　glad ;
Food for the famishing, jaded and spent ;
Strength for the stricken, the broken, the
　bent ;
Calm for the dying, where life nears the end,
"Lo, *I* am with you, thy Saviour and
　Friend."

"Lo, I am with you!" Sentence of bliss !
Where can the heart find an equal to this ?
Staff for all valleys,—and stay for all days,—
His promised presence for all of life's ways ;
Pillow to rest upon ; soft couch as well ;
Words whose full wondrousness lips cannot
　tell ;
"Lo, I am with you,"—words all sublime ;—
Great words, which change not ; unfaded by
　time.

" Lo, I am with you ! " He who all made,—
Who, by His blood, sin's great debt fully
      paid,—
'Tis He who said it,—His word abides true,
" Lo, I am with you ! " Lo, I am *with* you.
" Lo, I *am* with you,—am with you to-day,
" Lo, *I* am with you," through all of life's
      way :
" *Lo*, I am with you ! " Stay,—think—'tis
      His word ;
" Lo, I am with you, thy Saviour, and Lord."

Ours to believe what He doth declare ;
Ours to receive it and feed on its fare ;
Ours to enjoy His dear company blest ;
Ours to experience wonderful rest.
His to unfold—both through things old and
      new,
" Lo, I am with you "—really is true ;
His just to shew us, as riseth each need,
" Lo, I am with you "—is blest food indeed !

" TOO TIRED TO PRAY "

" Thou knowest my down-sitting and mine uprising : Thou understandest my thought afar off."—Psalm cxxxix. 2.

" ' I'M too tired to trust and too tired to
   pray,'
      Said one, as the overtaxed strength
      gave way.
' The one conscious thought by my mind
   possessed,
Is, Oh, could I just drop it all and rest.

Will God forgive me, do you suppose,
If I go right to sleep as a baby goes,
Without an asking if I may,
Without ever trying to trust and pray ? '

' Will God forgive you ? Why, think, dear
   heart,
When language to you was an unknown art,
Did a mother deny you needed rest,
Or refuse to pillow you on her breast ?

Did she let you want when you could not
   ask ?
Did she set her child an unequal task ?
Or did she cradle you in her arms,
And then guard your slumber against alarms ?

Oh ! how quick was her mother-love to see
The unconscious yearnings of infancy.
When you've grown too tired to trust and
    pray,
When over-wrought nature has quite given
    way,

Then just drop it all, and give up to rest,
As you used to do on a mother's breast.
He knows all about it—the dear Lord knows,
So just go to sleep as a baby goes,

Without even asking if you may,
God knows when His child is too tired to pray,
He judges not solely by uttered prayer,
He knows when the yearnings of love are
    there.

He knows you *do* pray, He knows you *do*
    trust,
And He knows, too, the limits of poor weak
    dust,
Oh, the wonderful sympathy of Christ,
For His chosen ones in that midnight tryst,

When He bade them sleep and take their rest,
While on Him the guilt of the whole world
    pressed.
—You've given your life up to Him to keep,
Then don't be afraid to go right to sleep.' "
                                        —*Anon.*

" WHEN I'M AFRAID "

By A. GARDNER

" *What time I am afraid, I will trust in Thee.*"—Psalm lvi. 3.

WHEN I'm afraid of times before,
　　What coming days will bring,
　　When life's omissions I deplore,
And earth-mists round me cling ;
O Lord of love, my weakness see,—
When I'm afraid I'll trust in Thee.

When I'm afraid of wily foes,
　　Their flattery and hate,—
Who seek my progress to oppose,—
　　My joys to dissipate ;
O Lord of hosts, my weakness see,—
When I'm afraid I'll trust in Thee.

When I'm afraid of dangers near,
　　Foreboding future ills ;
When rocks, and shoals, and deeps I fear,
　　And gloom my spirit fills ;
O Lord of might, my weakness see,—
When I'm afraid I'll trust in Thee.

When I'm afraid of crushing loss,
 Parting from loved ones dear,—
Lest I shall murmur at my cross,
 And yield to faithless fear ;
O Lord of peace, my weakness see,—
When I'm afraid I'll trust in Thee.

When I'm afraid of failing health,
 Sore weaknesses I know,—
And illness steals o'er me by stealth
 And sickness lays me low ;
O Lord of power, my weakness see,—
When I'm afraid I'll trust in Thee.

When I'm afraid of drear old age,
 As nature's powers decay,—
Mortality's dread heritage,
 Increasing day by day ;
O Lord of grace, my weakness see,—
When I'm afraid I'll trust in Thee.

" HE HAD TIME "

HE kept his soul unspotted
 As he went upon his way,—
And he tried to do some service
 For God's people, day by day.

He had time to cheer the doubter
 Who complained that hope was dead ;
He had time to help the cripple,
 When the way was rough ahead.

He had time to guard the orphan ;—
 And, one day,—well satisfied
With the talents God had given him,
 He closed his eyes and died.

He had time to see the beauty
 That the Lord spread all around ;
He had time to hear the music
 In the shells the children found ;

He had time to keep repeating,
 As he bravely worked away,—
" It is splendid to be living
 In the splendid world to-day ! "

But the crowds—the crowds that hurry
 After golden prizes—said
That " he never had succeeded,"
 When the clods lay o'er his head ;—

He had " dreamed,"—" he was a failure,"
 They compassionately sighed,
For the man had little money
 In his pockets when he died. *—Anon.*

" THE REFINER'S FIRE "

" He shall sit . . . and . . . purify the sons of Levi."—Mal. iii. 3.

NOTE.—" The refiner *sits* before the crucible, fixing his eyes on the metal, taking care that the heat is not too great, and keeping the metal in only until, by seeing his own image reflected in the glowing mass, he knows that the dross is completely consumed."—*Bible Dictionary*.

HE sat by a furnace of sevenfold heat,
   As He watched by the precious ore ;
   And closer He bent with a searching
      gaze,
As He heated it more and more.

He knew He had one that could stand the
     test,
   And He wanted the finest gold
To mould a crown for the King to wear,
   Set with gems of price untold.

So He laid our gold on the burning fire,
   Though we fain would say Him nay ;
And He watched the dross which we had not
     seen,
   As it melted and passed away.

And the gold grew brighter, and yet more
    bright,—
  But our eyes were so dim with tears ;
We saw but the fire—not the Master's
    hand,—
  And questioned with anxious fears.

Yet our gold shone out with a richer glow,
  As it mirrored a form above
That bent o'er the fire, though unseen by us,
  With a look of ineffable love.

Can we think it pleased His loving heart
  To cause us a moment's pain ?
Ah no ! But He saw through the furnace
    fierce
  The bliss of eternal gain.

So He waited there with a watchful eye,
  With a love that is strong and sure ;
And His gold did not suffer a whit more heat
  Than was needed to make it pure.

                        —Anon.

" THE THINGS I MISS "

AN easy thing, O Power Divine,
　　To thank Thee for these gifts of Thine ;
　　　For　summer's　sunshine, — winter's
　　　　snow,—
For hearts that kindle, thoughts that glow ;
But when shall I attain to this—
To thank Thee for the things I miss ?

For all young fancy's early gleams,—
The dreamed-of joys that still are dreams ;
Hopes unfulfilled, and pleasures known
Through others' fortunes, not my own ;
And blessings seen that are not given,
And ne'er will be this side of Heaven.

Had I, too, shared the joys I see,
Would there have been a Heaven for me ?
Could I have felt Thy presence near
Had I possessed what I held dear ?
My deepest fortune, highest bliss,
Have grown, perchance, from things I miss.

Sometimes there comes an hour of calm ;
Griefs turn to blessings, pain to balm :
A Power that works above my will
Still leads me onward, upward still :
And then my heart attains to this—
To thank Thee for the things I miss.

—Anon.

" CONTRASTING OUTLOOKS."

TWO men toiled side by side, from sun to
    sun,
      And both were poor ;
Both sat with children, when the day was
    done,
      About their door.

One saw the beautiful in crimson cloud,
      And shining moon ;
The other, with his head in sadness bowed,
      Made night of noon.

One loved each tree, and flower, and singing
    bird,
      On mount or plain ;
No music in the soul of one was stirred,
      By leaf or rain.

One saw the good in every fellow-man,
      And hoped the best ;
The other marvelled at his Master's plan,
      And doubt confessed.

One, having heaven above, and heaven below,
      Was satisfied ;
The other, discontented, lived in woe,
      And hopeless died.

                        —*Anon.*

" MINE——OR HIS ? "

I OWNED a little boat a while ago,—
  And sailed a morning sea without a fear ;
  And whither any breeze might fairly blow,
I steered my little craft afar or near.
    Mine was the boat ; and mine the air ;
    And mine the sea ; nor mine a care.

My boat became my place of nightly toil ;
I sailed at sunset to the fishing ground :
At morn the boat was freighted with the spoil
That my all-conquering work and skill had
        found.
    Mine was the boat ; and mine the net ;
    And mine the skill and power to get.

One day there passed along the silent shore,—
While I my net was casting in the sea,
A man, who spake as never man before.
I followed Him,—new life began in me.
    Mine was the boat,—but His the voice ;
    And His the call ; yet mine the choice.

Oh, 'twas a fearful night out on the lake,—
And all my skill availed not at the helm
Till Him, asleep, I wakened, crying,—" Take,
Take Thou command, lest water overwhelm."
    His was the boat ; and His the sea ;
    And His the peace o'er all and me.

Once from His boat He taught the curious
    throng,
Then bade me let down nets out in the sea.
I murmured, but obeyed ; nor was it long
Before the catch amazed and humbled me.
  His was the boat,—and His the skill,
  And His the catch, and His my will.
                      —*Anon.*

" GRACE "

GRACE when the sun is shining, Lord ;
   Grace when the sky is black ;
   Grace when I get the unkind word ;
Grace on the too smooth track.
Grace when I'm elbowed into a nook ;
   Grace when I get my turn ;
Grace when the dinner will not cook ;
   Grace when the fire won't burn.

Grace when my duties go all wrong ;
   Grace when they seem all right ;
Grace when 'tis gladness, praise, and song ;
   Grace when I have to fight.
Grace when my dress is fresh and new ;
   Grace when it's worn and old ;
Grace when my purse is empty, too ;
   Grace when it's full of gold.

Grace when the saved ones don't act saved,
   And lay all the blame on me ;
Grace when the grace I've asked and craved
   Seems denied to me, Lord, by Thee.
Grace when the midnight hours I tell ;
   Grace when the morn is nigh ;
Grace when I'm healthy, strong, and well ;
   Grace when I come to die.

—Anon.

"THE RED SEA PLACE"

By ANNIE JOHNSON FLINT

———

" By the greatness of Thine arm they shall be still . . . till Thy people pass over, O Lord."—Exod. xv. 16.

———

HAVE you come to the Red Sea place in
     your life,
    Where, in spite of all you can do,
There is no way out, there is no way back,
    There is no other way but—through?
Then wait on the Lord, with a trust serene,
    Till the night of your fear is gone ;
He will send the wind,—He will heap the
    floods,
    When He says to your soul, " Go on."

And His hand will lead you through—clear
    through—
    Ere the watery walls roll down ;
No foe can reach you, no wave can touch,
    No mightiest sea can drown :
The tossing billows may rear their crests,
    Their foam at your feet may break,—
But over their bed you shall walk dry shod,
    In the path that your Lord will make.

In the morning watch,—'neath the lifted
  cloud,—
  You shall see but the Lord alone,—
When He leads you on from the place of the
  sea
  To a land that you have not known ;
And your fears shall pass, as your foes have
  passed,
  You shall no more be afraid ;
You shall sing His praise in a better place,—
  A place that His hand has made.

—*By per. Evangelical Publishers.*

" THE MAT "

By H. Suso.

(*Isaiah l.* 6.)

IT was on a winter's morning,
   In the days of old ;
  In his cell sat Father Henry,
   Sorrowful and cold.

" O my Lord, I am aweary,"
   In his heart he spake,
" For my brethren scorn and hate me
   For Thy blessed sake.

" If I had but one to love me,
   That were joyful cheer—
One small word to make me sunshine
   Through the darksome year !

" But they mock me and despise me,
   Till my heart is stung ;
Then my words are wild and bitter,
   Tameless is my tongue."

Then the Lord said, " I am with thee ;
   Trust thyself to Me ;
Open thou thy little casement,
   Mark what thou shalt see."

Then a piteous look and wistful
   Father Henry cast
Out into the dim old cloister,
   And the wintry blast.

Was it that a friend was coming,
   By some angel led ?
No ! a great hound, wild and savage,
   Round the cloister sped.

Some old mat, that lay forgotten,
    Seized he on his way—
Tore it, tossed it, dragged it wildly
    Round the cloister gray.

" Lo, the hound is like thy brethren,"
    Spake the Voice he knew ;
" If thou art the mat, belovéd,
    What hast thou to do ? "

Meekly then went Father Henry,
    And the mat he bare
To his little cell, to store it
    As a jewel rare.

Many a winter and a summer,
    Through those cloisters dim,
Did he thenceforth walk rejoicing,
    And the Lord with him.

And when bitter words would sting him,
    Turned he to his cell,
Took his mat, and looked upon it,
    Saying, " All is well.

" He who is the least and lowest
    Needs but low to lie ;
Lord, I thank Thee and I praise Thee
    That the *mat* am I."

Then he wept,—for in the stillness
    His Belovéd spake,
" Thus was I the least and lowest,
    Gladly, for thy sake.

" Lo, My face to shame and spitting
    Did I turn for thee ;
If thou art the least and lowest,
    Then remember Me."

"IN THE FOURTH WATCH"

By IVY M. FORDHAM

" *He constrained His disciples to get into the ship.
. . . And when even was come, the ship was in the
midst of the sea, and He alone on the land.   And He
saw them toiling in rowing. . . .* "—Mark vi. 45-48.

" *And it was now dark, and Jesus was not come to
them.   And the sea arose by reason of a great wind
that blew. . . .* "—John vi. 17, 18.

" *And about the fourth watch of the night He cometh
unto them. . . .* "—Mark vi. 48.

" *Then they willingly received Him into the ship :
and immediately the ship was at the land whither they
went.*"—John vi. 21.

O'ER Galilee the pall of night was falling,
    The stormy sunset faded from the sky,
    And angry clouds piled up, while gusts of fury
        Lashed at the restless waves to lift them
           high.
On the bleak shore there stood one lonely Figure
    Gazing far out to where, against the tide,
Tossed the small boat, in which His twelve disciples
    Toiled in their rowing t'ward the other side.

Yet, *He* had sent them out into the tempest,
    Knowing all they would feel of anguished fear.
Oh, wondrous Love, that, passing human knowledge,
    Dares thus to test the ones He holds most dear !
With yearning heart He watched the gale grow
    wilder,
    Saw their distress—and then He turned away,
And, climbing up the lonely mountain pathway,
    He sought His Father, there to watch and pray.

The night wore on, and fiercer grew the conflict,
    Higher the waves, more boisterous the wind ;
And in the boat, a horror of great darkness
    Rested upon each weary heart and mind.

Worse than the storm, more fearful than the
    tempest,
  Lay the dark doubt that He Who let them go,
Must have forsaken them, else why this silence ?
  Did He not *care*,—for surely He must know.

Oh, the long hours, when, flickering hope extin-
    guished,
  Still they fought on with death and dark despair !
Through the first watch, and, weary, through the
    second ;
  Then through the third, and *still* He was not there.
On wears the night, and yet the Master tarries,
  High on the mountain, wrapt in earnest prayer :
Does He not know, nor feel for those worn toilers,
  Or will He test them more than they can bear ?

Comes the fourth watch, and lo, upon the waters,
  In the grey dawn, there moves a distant form !
" Who can *this* be ? " they cry in sore amazement—
  Is it a ghost, more awful than the storm ?
Listen ! He speaks ! Above the tempest's raging
  His voice rings out, so welcome to their ears—
" Be not afraid, for it is I, your Master "—
  Oh, how it drives away all doubts and fears.

Still the storm rages, but what care they for it ?
  Has not their Loved One seen and come to save ?
All through the testing He has known their sorrow,
  What matters now the wind, the mighty wave ?
E'en as He steps into the boat, it steadies ;
  All the wild noise is hushed, the billows sleep ;
Lo, they have reached the seeming-distant landing,
  And the bright sun is rising o'er the deep.

Oh, child of God, pressed down in awful conflict,
  Seeing no light, the heavens like as brass,—
Think you your Lord knows not, or has not
    measured
  The depths through which He causes you to pass ?
Do not despair, for, loving you most dearly,
  He intercedes for you before the Throne :
Though long and dark the night, and fierce the
    tempest,
  In the fourth watch He cometh to His own.

"GOD UNDERSTANDETH"

By M. COLLEY

———

(*Job xxviii*. 23.)

———

GOD understandeth thy trouble and care,
　　Sees when the burden seems grievous
　　　　to bear ;
God understandeth when false grows a
　　friend—
　　He, and He only, is true to the end.

God understandeth each thought of thy
　　heart :
　　Knows why and wherefore the sudden tears
　　　　start ;
Feels, oh ! so keenly, thy trouble and grief,
　　Longing intensely to give thee relief.

Cast thyself, then, on His wonderful love,
　　He will uphold thee with strength from
　　　　above ;
Yield Him *thyself*, He will do all the rest,—
　　God understandeth, and God knoweth best.

" UNANSWERED YET ? "

By —— BROWNING

UNANSWERED yet—the prayer your
   lips have pleaded,
   In agony of heart these many years ?
Does faith begin to fail ? Is hope departing ?
  And think you all in vain those falling
    tears ?
Say not the Father hath not heard your
    prayer ;
You shall have your desire,—sometime,—
    somewhere.

Unanswered yet ? Though when you first
    presented
  This one petition at the Father's throne,
It seemed you could not wait the time of
    asking,
  So urgent was your heart to make it known.
Though years have passed since then, do not
    despair ;
The Lord will answer you,—sometime,—
    somewhere.

Unanswered yet ? Nay, do not say " un-
    granted " ;
  Perhaps *your* part is not yet wholly done :
The work began when first your prayer was
    uttered,—
  And God will finish what He has begun.

If you will keep the incense burning There,
His glory you shall see,—sometime,—some-
    where.

Unanswered yet ? Faith cannot be un-
    answered !
  Her feet were firmly planted on the Rock :
Amid the wildest storms she stands un-
    daunted,—
  Nor quails before the loudest thunder-
    shock.
She knows Omnipotence has heard her
    prayer,—
And cries—" It shall be done,—sometime,—
    somewhere."

" JUST TO BE HAPPY IN JESUS "

By ANNIE LIND-WOODWORTH.

JUST to be happy in Jesus,
    And meet every fear with faith's song ;
  This is my daily commission,
Though everything seems to go wrong.

Just to be restful in Jesus,
  Though often with thorns I am tried ;
Quietly in Him confiding,—
  Content, since with Him I abide.

Just to be hopeful in Jesus,
  When sorrows and troubles abound ;
Sharing with others the gladness,—
  The joy in the Lord I have found.

Just to be thankful for all things,—
  This is my Father's sweet will ;
Knowing that all work together
  God's purpose in me to fulfil.

" THE PEACE OF TRIUMPH "

" The peace of God, which passeth all understanding."—Phil. iv. 7.

" My peace I give unto you."—John xiv. 27.

" Father, if Thou be willing, remove this cup from Me : nevertheless not My will, but Thine, be done."—Luke xxii. 42.

THERE is a peace that cometh after
    sorrow,—
    Of hope surrendered, not of hope
      fulfilled ;
A peace that looketh not upon the morrow,—
    But calmly on a tempest that is stilled.

A peace that lives not now in joy's excesses,—
    Nor in the happy life of love secure,—
But in the unerring strength the heart
      possesses
    Of conflicts won, while learning to endure.

A peace there is, in sacrifice secluded,—
    A life subdued,—from will and passion
      free ;
'Tis not the peace that over Eden brooded,
    But that which triumphed in Gethsemane.
                   ANON.

" LET HIM "
By J. DANSON SMITH

SIMPLE words,—yet key to blessing
 Richer far than speech can tell :
Free to all His name confessing,
In whose hearts He thus doth dwell.

For within each true believer
 Jesus lives,—would live in power,
Longing that He may deliver
 Each one in temptation's hour.

When within hot words are burning,
 Stinging words,—which rankle sore,
Only " let Him " bear the spurning,
 Thus to find it stings no more.

When *your* patience ends completely
 With the things that go all wrong,
Only " let Him "—He can sweetly
 Bear with these things, oh, so long.

When your ruffled heart feels fretting
 At the pin-pricks and the stings,
" Let Him " bear these, not forgetting
 He can triumph o'er such things.

When those feelings,—rushed, exciting,
 Rob you of your inward rest,
" Let Him " keep—your look inviting
 Him to reign within your breast.

When that *driven* sense keeps urging,
 And you almost frantic grow ;
" Let Him " meet that inward scourging,
 He can quench the strongest foe.

When the ceaseless tasks keep pressing,
  And you almost would complain,
" Let Him " then meet all depressing
  Sense of burdenedness and pain.

When unhallowed thoughts are filling,
  Aye, and fouling, too, your heart,—
Then be simple, yes, and *willing*
  To " let Him " bid them depart.

When your lonely heart feels breaking
  O'er some cause for deepest grief,
" Let Him " then subdue the aching,
  Let Him *in* to give relief.

When, if called, to tell the story
  Of the One who for us died,
Shrink not back,—tell for His glory,
  Just " let Him " the power provide.

When to higher height He leadeth,
  Asking that you yield up all,
" Let Him " meet all your heart needeth
  To respond to such a call.

When His Word speaks, surely, gravely,
  That some things be cleansed away,
Do not fear,—but face all bravely,—
  " Let Him " and His Word have sway.
   *   *   *   *
Key to blessing, rich in measure,—
  Key to rest in time of strife,
Key to wondrous inward treasure,
  Key to a triumphant life ;—

Not our copy of His goodness,
  Be that copy passing fair,
But just " letting Him " within us
  All things meet and all things bear.

" DELIVERED "
By M. Colley

" Who hath *delivered us from the power of darkness, and* hath *translated us into the kingdom of His dear Son."*—Col. i. 13.

DO you feel a cloud of darkness,
   Black as night, upon you now,—
   Pressing closer every moment,
     While, to pray, you know not how?
Even God Himself seems distant,—
Everything all wrapped in gloom,—
While a terror of the future
   Grips you like a living tomb?

Listen, then,—HE *" hath* delivered
   Us "—(and that means me and you),
Not alone from " darkness " only,
   But from *" power* of darkness," too :
He hath set us free from terrors,
   And translated us, instead,
To HIS kingdom and HIS keeping ;
   We need have no further dread !

" It is finished " !   Claim it therefore !
   Lift your eyes unto the light ;
All your gloomy fears shall vanish,
   As the sunshine follows night.
For the darkness hath no power
   O'er the soul uplifted thus :
Glory be to God our Father,
   That HE *hath* delivered us !

" HOPE'S SONG "

*" The Lord blessed the latter end of Job
more than his beginning."*—Job. xlii. 12.

*" . . . what He hath prepared for him that
waiteth for Him."*—Is. lxiv. 4.

*" Eye hath not seen, nor ear heard, neither
have entered into the heart of man, the things
which God hath prepared for them that love
Him."*—I Co. ii. 9.

I HEAR it singing, singing sweetly,
   Softly in an undertone,—
  Singing as if God had taught it,
    " It is better farther on ! "

Night and day it sings the same song,
   Sings it while I sit alone,
Sings so that the heart may hear it,
    " It is better farther on ! "

Sits upon the grave and sings it,
   Sings it when the heart would groan,
Sings it when the shadows darken,
    " It is better farther on ! "

Farther on ?   Oh, how much farther ?
   Count the milestones one by one.
No, not counting, only trusting,
    " It is better farther on ! "

—Selected.

" MORE THAN CONQUERORS ! "
By ELIZA CRAWFURD

" In all these things we are more than conquerors through HIM *that loved us."—*
Rom. viii. 37.

MORE than conqueror ! Can it be ?
Lord, is this possible for me ?
   A life triumphant here to know,
Amidst earth's tumult, pain, and woe ?
That over Satan, self, and sin,
I may, in EVERY conflict, win ?

Yes, My dear child, it is indeed,—
For I will give you all you need ;
I overcame the world for thee
That ye might overcome in Me.
The world may sneer, and Satan frown,—
Yet none need rob thee of thy crown.

Then, Lord, in Thy beloved name,—
By faith, Thy promise now I claim ;
To know in weakness, perfect strength ;
Thy love, its height, depth, breadth and
    length ;
That Thou wilt henceforth, hour by hour,
Show forth in me Thy love and power.

My child, thou shalt have thy desire !
'Twas I who did thy soul inspire
To seek a closer walk with Me
In undisturbed tranquility.
Be of good cheer,—still trust in Me,—
And more than conqueror thou shalt be.

" PRESSED "

By Louise S. Pridgeon.

PRESSED out of measure and pressed to
all length ;
   Pressed so intensely, it seems beyond
   strength ;
Pressed in the body, and pressed in the soul,
Pressed in the mind till the dark surges roll ;
Pressed by my foes, sorely pressed by my
   friends ;
Pressure on pressure, till life nearly ends.

Pressed into knowing no helper but God ;
Pressed into loving the staff and the rod.
Pressed into liberty, where nothing clings ;
Pressed into faith for impossible things.
Pressed into living a life in the Lord ;
Pressed into living a Christ-life outpoured.

" FOR THIS HE WAITS "

By HARRY J. PREECE

O SAVIOUR Christ ! for many years I
    failed
    To understand what Thou to men
      would'st be ;
Thy truth I held, Thy promises I loved,
    Thy service prized, yet little knew of Thee.

O Living Lord ! Thyself the Word of God,
    The very Bread of Heaven—broken small !
Revealed to me, within, I know Thee now :
    Thou art my Life, and Thou would'st be
      my All !

Thy truth is dear, Thy word of promise sure :
    To know and hold Thy truth worth more
      than gold ;
But now 'tis Thee I prize—Thyself the
    Truth !
    Thyself the Living Word I love and hold !

And knowing Thee, when trial and sorrow
    press,
    When nerves are weary, or the body weak,
I do not *try* to think, or *try* to pray,
    But rest in Thee with love that need not
      speak.

When, Lord, at times the sterner call doth
    come
  To stand all-armed and fight 'gainst hell
    and sin,
My Armour then art Thou—in Thee I stand,
  Whilst Thou, Thyself, dost guard my heart
    within.

When days of gloom, with mist and sweeping
    rain,
  Obscure the trusted landmarks of my soul,
And faith and hope seem dead, e'en then I
    know
  Thou still art surely guiding t'ward the
    Goal !

.   .   .   .   .

Oh, teach us, Lord, to look through all to Thee :
  To rest not e'en in Scripture, faith, or
    prayers,
But rest in Thee—in Thee, Thyself ! and then
  To love Thee back with love that clings and
    dares !

.   .   .   .   .

For this He waits, and through the Spirit
    works :
  He yearns to be our " meat and drink
    indeed " ;
And naught but this will satisfy His love,
  As naught but this can satisfy our need.

" THE END OF THE WAY "

By HARRIET COLE.

MY life is a wearisome journey,
　　I am sick of the dust and the heat;
　　　The rays of the sun beat upon me,
　　The briers are wounding my feet ;
But the City to which I am going,
　　Will more than my trials repay ;
　　　The toils of the road will be nothing,
　　　When I get to the end of the way.

There are so many hills to climb upward,
　　I often am longing for rest ;
But He Who appoints me my pathway
　　Knows just what is needful and best :
I know in His Word He has promised
　　My strength shall be as my day ;
　　　The toils of the road will be nothing,
　　　When I get to the end of the way.

He loves me too well to forsake me,
　　Or give me one trial too much ;
All His people have been dearly purchased,
　　And Satan can never claim such.
By and by I shall see Him, and praise Him,
　　In the land of unending day ;
　　　The toils of the road will be nothing,
　　　When I get to the end of the way.

Though often I'm weary and footsore,
    I shall rest when I'm safely at home ;
I know I'll receive a glad welcome,
    For the Saviour Himself has said " Come."
So, whenever my trials seem heavy,
    And I'm sinking in spirit, I say :—
        The toils of the road will be nothing,
        When I get to the end of the way.

Cool fountains are there for the thirsty,
    And cordials for those who are faint ;
And robes that are purer and whiter
    Than any that fancy can paint.
So I'll try to press hopefully onward,
    Thinking often through each weary day,
        The toils of the road will be nothing,
        When I get to the end of the way.

When the last feeble step has been taken,
    And the gates of the City appear,
And the beautiful songs of the angels
    Float out on my listening ear ;
Then all that now seems so mysterious
    Will be plain and clear as the day,
        Oh, the toils of the road will be
        NOTHING,
        When I get to the end of the way.

" AT LAST "

By JOHN GREENLEAF WHITTIER

WHEN on my day of life the night is
falling,
And, in the winds, from unsunned
spaces blown,
I hear far voices, out of darkness calling
My feet to paths unknown,

Thou who hast made my home of life so
pleasant,
Leave not its tenant when its walls decay ;
O Love Divine, O Helper ever present,
Be Thou my strength and stay !

Be near me when all else from me is drifting :
Earth, sky, home's pictures, days of shade
and shine,
And kindly faces to my own uplifting
The love which answers mine.

I have but Thee, my Father ! let Thy spirit
Be with me then to comfort and uphold ;
No gate of pearl, no branch of palm I merit,
Nor street of shining gold.

Suffice it if—my good and ill unreckoned,
And both forgiven through Thy abounding
grace—
I find myself by hands familiar beckoned
Unto my fitting place.

Some humble door among Thy many man-
    sions,—
  Some sheltering shade where sin and
    striving cease,—
And flows forever through Heaven's green
    expansions
  The river of Thy peace.

There, from the music round about me
    stealing,
  I fain would learn the new and holy song,
And find at last, beneath Thy trees of healing,
  The life for which I long.

"THE LITTLE SHARP VEXATIONS"

By REV. PHILIPS BROOKS.

THE little sharp vexations,
    And the briers that catch and fret,
  Why not take them all to the Helper
  Who has never failed us yet?

Tell Him about the heart-ache,
  And tell Him the *longings* too,—
Tell Him the baffled purpose
  When we scarce know what to do.

Then leaving all, with our weakness,
  With the One divinely strong,
Forget that we bore the burden,
  And carry away the song.

"THE LIGHT THAT IS FELT"

By JOHN GREENLEAF WHITTIER.

A TENDER child of summers three,
　　Seeking her little bed at night,
　　Paused on the dark stair timidly.
　"Oh, Mother! Take my hand," said
　　she,—
　"And then the dark will all be light."

We older children grope our way
　From dark behind to dark before ;
And only when our hands we lay,
　Dear Lord, in Thine, the night is day,—
　And there is darkness nevermore.

Reach downward to the sunless days,
　Wherein our guides are blind as we,—
And faith is small, and hope delays ;
　Take Thou the hands of prayer we raise,
　And let us feel the light of Thee !

"ONWARD GO!"

By EDWIN R. MILES

" Let us go on."—Heb. vi. 1.

PRAY on, pray on, dear pilgrims! God
hears and answers prayer!
He'll lighten every burden, He'll drive
away your care.
Pray on, pray on, ne'er ceasing, pray with
thanksgiving, too,
There's much to own of goodness, God is so
good and true.

Work on, work on, dear pilgrims! the need
is truly great!
The fields are white to harvest; work ere it
be too late.
Be stedfast and unmoving, abounding day by
day,
His grace is all sufficient, however rough the
way.

Sing on, sing on, dear pilgrims! then sighing
will depart!
The song which gladdens others, will cheer
your weary heart.
Sing songs of joy and gladness, this world is
full of woe,
Sing in the shade or sunshine, sing every-
where you go.

Wait on, wait on, dear pilgrims ! the time is
     drawing near,
When labours will be ended, and Christ will
     re-appear ;
Our eyes shall then behold him, we'll see His
     blessed face,
And tell with hearts enraptured, the story of
     His grace.

Press on, press on, dear pilgrims ! the *upward*
     way leads Home !
The wilderness or desert is only " Till He
     Come."
The past is all forgiven, the future fair and
     bright :
Soon, soon will be the " Welcome," and
     ended be the night.

Cheer up, cheer up, dear pilgrims ! oft tried
     with griefs and pain !
We must, through tribulations, the Heavenly
     glory gain.
The suff'ring of this present, compared can
     never be
With glories that shall follow, through all
     eternity.

" KEEP UP THE SONG OF FAITH "

By M. E. BARBER.

" *With my song will I praise Him.*"—
Psalm xxviii. 7.

" *I will praise the name of God with a
song.*"—Psalm lxix. 30.

" *My song in the night.*"—Psalm lxxvii. 6.

" *Thy statutes have been my song in the
house of my pilgrimage.*"—Psalm cxix. 54.

KEEP up the song of faith,
　　However dark the night ;
　　And, as you praise, the Lord will work
To change your faith to sight.

Keep up the song of faith,
　　And let your heart be strong,—
For God delights when faith can praise
　　Though dark the night and long.

Keep up the song of faith ;
　　The foe will hear and flee :
Oh, LET NOT SATAN HUSH YOUR SONG ;
　　For *praise is victory.*

Keep up the song of faith ;
　　The dawn will break ere long ;
And we shall go to meet the Lord,
　　And join the endless song.